A HISTORY
of YEARNING

for Pat –
thank you + all appreciation
+ best of luck w. your writing
Kathleen

A History *of* Yearning

∞

poems

∞

Kathleen Spivack

Kathleen Spivack
Salem 2015

The 2009 Sow's Ear Chapbook
Competition Winner

ACKNOWLEDGMENTS

Thanks to the editors of the following publications, where some of the poems in this collection appeared originally:

Agni: "Penelope"
Kansas Quarterly: "Monet's 'Path'"
Madison Review: "Earth's Burnt Umber"
Oberon: "Women Wearing White"
Society of Fellows, American Academy of Rome Newsletter: "Owl Cry Over Rome"
Southern California Anthology: "Photographs Already Fading"
Spoon River Poetry Review: "Open Studio: Landscape Paintings" "Tipping Point"
The Atlantic Monthly: "The Path Into Night"
The Laurel Review: "Watercolor"
The Southern Review: "Pale Light in the Luxembourg Garden"

Text copyright © 2010 by Kathleen Spivack. Issued as Vol. XX, No. 1, of *The Sow's Ear Poetry Review*. All rights reserved. No part of this chapbook may be reproduced in any manner whatsoever without the permission of the publisher, except in the case of quotations in reviews or articles. *The Sow's Ear Poetry Review* is a component of The Word Process, a not-for-profit corporation chartered in Virginia. Information is available from Robert G. Lesman, Managing Editor, THE SOW'S EAR POETRY REVIEW, P.O. Box 127, Millwood, VA, 22646, and at http://sows-ear.kitenet.net.

First Edition, May, 2010

Cover design by SIJIE WANG & MARIN SPIVACK

ISSN 1535-5462

Contents

1. A History of Yearning

Night Hawks	1
After Night Hawks. Hopper. 1942.	2
A History of Yearning	4
Monet's "Path"	5
Penelope	6
Open Studio: Landscape Paintings	7

2. Earth's Burnt Umber

Photographs Already Fading	11
Earth's Burnt Umber	14
Women Wearing White	16
That Light. That Photograph. That Couple.	17
Watercolor	18

3. The Lost World

The Lost World	21
Pale Light in the Luxembourg Garden	23
Their Tranquil Lives	24
MOMA. New York City	26
Owl Cry Over Rome	28
Tipping Point	29
Button	30
The Path Into Night	31

A History of Yearning

#1. NIGHT HAWKS. 1942.

What are they doing there, strangers,
under the pitiless arc of a light
bulb, sitting together as if it mattered,
alone in a late-night café in New York?
One would do anything not to go home

tonight. Outside, it is not yet raining,
thick city, that one misty
streetlight. *"Going home"* means
lying awake; the yawn
and yawp of it, like death.

In the bar, they are speaking as if
conversation mattered, as if thought or
speculation counted for anything under
the brief umbrella that *is our life*—or *lives*—
Pour us another cup of coffee, counter-
man. Outside this dim-lit circle,
sparked by occasional utterance
lies the darker destiny of *leaving*.

Beyond the all-night refuge, New York
City, lies America abandoned
to its waiting silences.
The land is vast, domed/doomed
and resonating, grooved
like the inside of a long train-
moan, funneled, crossing &
re-crossing the prairie,

its withdrawing cry of *lonely*
briefly waking sleepers
where the track runs
next to dreams. The after-sound
unfurls the banner
of the plains, their little sleepy
towns, the whistle-stops;
the trains long warning and
its terrible goodbyes:

soon it will be closing time.
Or just before.

#2. After Night Hawks. Hopper. 1942.

Why *Night Hawks*,
dropped down for the kill
as if on surveillance missions,
instead of *Night Owls, 1942?*
The yellow wedge of light,
jutting, ship's prow, toward
a future—as if there were one
for these civilians lost
in greenish isolation
in this New York late-
night diner.

The *"strumpet"*—or so she must be
since she is wearing red—sits,
lost in contemplation of how
she ended up in this dive anyway;
and the depressed stranger alongside,
morose over his cigarettes so
late at night, ponders the same.

There is another—isn't there always?—
a *"third man,"* watching with
equal parts of suspicion and envy
from the far edge of the painting,
concealed as is usual,
half in darkness, his
bulbous right ear cocked &
illuminated.

What are they all doing there, seeking
refuge while the war goes on?
You might almost say they are
refugees—from history—
from themselves, from night, their
fear apparent beneath nonchalance.
I've lived with a World War Two
veteran myself: his war, stoic &
compulsory, always present in our lives
like the neighborhood cat
pressing against us in the shadows.

Back then the light was a
blazing streak of bold yellow,
the torch that defined each
scene, half-lived, since 1942.
Beyond the liberty ships lay
darkness & minefields,
and the idealistic sailors fished
the others from the water:
their freighted upturned bodies
like stone carvings of bishops
laid on their own tombs,
riding to shore.

Tonight the optimistic
counterman proffers coffee.
He is young, blond, hopeful
as if his service mattered:
the hero we have been
waiting for; listening, helpful;
leans forward, an Angel with promises,
gold hair, white coat & jaunty hat.
His coffee machines are gleaming:
he doesn't even smoke, he is so pure.

All in this diner, with its decorative
sign *Phillies* viewed from outside
as from heaven, are frozen
before their perhaps
untarnished destinies.
The color "*blood*," its sharp
metallic smear, is yet to
appear in this picture. In
Edward Hopper's painting,
Night Hawks 1942, the man
with his back to us, waiting, half-
lit, has already figured this out.

A History of Yearning

For air, for breath when we didn't
know we were gasping—
like the too-large swimming pool in
a David Hockney painting.
How casual the figures seem,
lounging about in their good
clothes, clink of cool glasses, hands and
how quickly they might assume
the sinewy flayed grimaces
of his contemporary, Sir Francis
Bacon. *(That "Sir": doesn't that
suggest the word "Carelessness?")*

Yet how we love paintings,
their endless vestibules to possibility
and airy aqua pleasures.
The David Hockney
"Swimming Pool" from his Los
Angeles period—you know, the one
that breaks all rules of perspective:
a light-limbed floating trapezoid
we are looking into as if from Above;
as if there were really a heaven.

Monet's "Path"

You walk into the painting,
you walk down the path
through the bleached grass toward the village:
the cicadas are singing;
you are going someplace

ordinary.
Perhaps it is to the post office,
perhaps it is to get milk;
the dry grasses are hardly stirring:
a museum guard is at standstill, watching you.

You walk next to poplar trees,
you walk through sun and shade:
it is an ordinary errand
but the flowers shriek, brighter than daytime,
and the weeds murmur: "notice me."

The painter is so much a part of this
the crickets hardly bother to silence themselves.
Nothing stops singing:
grass celebrates its green-ness
and the moist ground, underfoot,

springs back, debonair, as
you part it with your eye—it is almost
a feeling—this green dapple of light and shade,
framed, dazzling, just when you entered it.

Penelope

The sea is forever running out, she said—
where does it run to?
The waves made frothy scallops on the shore:
she might try to hold each one in her eye
but another, lace upon lace, came to undo
what she so carefully wove.
She had been waiting for so long she had forgotten
the answer to the yearning she was working for.
Who can remember the difficult embroidery
when each day's blue-green tapestry unfolds:
a field, flung out, upon which to emblazon
a coat of arms?
"A life. My life." The words,
whispered aloud, were ludicrous.
The quick lizards skittered and the reeds
crackled with auguries:
"Forget, forget," murmured the waves,
stitching themselves round her ankles.
Caressing her, they undid the pattern.

OPEN STUDIO: LANDSCAPE PAINTINGS

for DLP
American Academy in Rome

These precise
enunciated landscapes:
each one to be floated
on river of eyesight, passing
the aureole halos of trees
saying "come in"; the paths
ending in faraway mist,
not the end of the road,
only what you could see
from it: cool shadows
brushed, soft breath-
on-skin like chartreuse
summer drawn toward
the vanishing point,
ambiguous and veiled;
that place we never really
leave. Forget frame,
forget canvas, forget
white walls and studio
and all the noiseful clutter,
preparations, putting
paintings up. Forget even
making them, or having
made, or being remade
by them. No rectangles
on walls, no barriers:
just the *"just-be"*
before the light
changed, darkened
lifetimes/afternoons/and
landscapes not meant to be entered;
the greendream shimmer
saying *this is how it was then,*
that moment, yes, it was like this.

Earth's Burnt Umber

Photographs Already Fading.

Part One. Grandcamp. February 2003

Sur les plages, les plages du débarquement
last night we could not sleep. We tried the hot
expressions: nothing worked.
The sea roared round Arromanches, bitten by
History: writhed, could not rid
itself *(rid itself)*, banging the shore.
We wanted only to be simple together
but History would not have it, would not lie down
quietly, great History, with its proud reputation.
(History defined as the study and listing of Wars:
occurrence, methods, tactics, generals, insurrections,
acquisitions, miscalculations, losses, costs,
cause and effects, impact upon, etcetera.)

It riddled our ears like the sea at Grandcamp:
we breathed the sharp air, the night prickled with stars
and the young men froze where they fell,
"Come to the window…"
Like a time-lapse of itself, stop-framed,
the odd tank, abandoned, will never rust;
"…whispering of fields half-sown,
Always it woke him, even in France…"
And the Maire, remembering, wakes up at 5 AM
to polish it anew. It squats immoveable in the center
of town by the Crêperie and the 'Monoprix.'

Sur les plages, les plages du débarquement
the young men lie where they fell.
They must stay by the sea, that terrible sea:
they will stay the same age as they were when they died
next to Normandy peasants whose small farms burned down
who stay the same age in their blouses of blue.
White hysterical chickens keep scattering, sheds collapse, beams
afire, women run about, hands clasped to mouths,

and that one lone parachutist
still dangles askew from the cocked-hat church steeple.

Photographs Already Fading

Part Two. Paris. March 2003

Sur le pont, le pont de la déportation

we walked across Paris to protest "war."
The specific war *(Iraq)* had not yet started.
We filed with the Americans and the French
(who wept, recalling "Libération");
past the Jewish Memorial to the Deportees,
the bridges, the skeletons, the polished plaques
to fallen heroes, the Armory, and the famously
untouched and self-regarding Notre Dame.

And we walked also in Melbourne in London in New
York *(not allowed to walk there, just to "stand")*
in Spain and Italy and Germany, Japan, Etcetera.
Back home the nineteen-year-old boys
were freezing their sperm,
just in case. They too were walking—
would be walking—elsewhere.

You were beside me, French and tall and noble,
and when it was over, the protest march I mean,
you took me for ice cream, whipped
cream, & coffee on the Isle St. Louis
at Berthillon, all velvet fringe, and chandeliers.
At the next table, two men joined us:
Saudi, American, in town for the weekend
attending a meeting of OPEC. We warmed
ourselves and spoke of politics and
war and *thought perhaps of private things*
overlooking glorious violet Paris
at Berthillon, magnificent with mango ices:
as from that soft red interior glow
the whole Isle St. Louis and the somber Seine,
spreading, darkened, coming alive.

By the Seine, the mysterious seen-it-all Seine.

Photographs Already Fading

Part Three. "Anthem for Doomed Youth" exhibit.
Imperial War Museum, London. January 2003

High up in the British Imperial War Museum
the crisp-voiced "World War One Poets"
bite "received" consonants, thanks to the Museum's rental
headphones. No rain today *"under an English heaven,"*
and the poems are read beautifully by contemporary actors.
Siegfried Sassoon, Wilfred Owen, Rupert
Brooke and Robert Graves, Blunden, Rosenberg
and others, petals pressed in glass, cohabit
near the galleries for "Instruments of War" and "Crimes Against
Humanity" upstairs. This squat Museum's much too large: it hulks.
Still it's a lovely day in London. The "Anthem for Doomed Youth"
is a gentlemanly dirge; the verse so sure
we can almost relax; hopeful these young poets were
at first, and eager, patriotic*: "…time for tea?"* and
"Everyone suddenly burst out singing…."
(*Until After. Was there ever an After?)*

Like perfectly sliced limes in aspic, letters
to their mothers are preserved in cases
as when photographs are taken underwater, idealized,
the scholar-warriors made more luminous by time.
They wave to us, frond-like, going down,
as if telling us something urgent, moving away….
"Horror of wounds and anger at the foe,
and loss of things desired…."
Their poems drown disillusionment and fear
in precise metric verse, so carefully
recorded: few are typed.
The crumpled papers are uncreased
for this occasion: they lie smooth.
Today rare winter English sunlight gilds the gallery,
glints off museum cases, glares aggressively.
Dust motes disturb. The scribbled letters blur;
the photos fade in their frames.
Stand slant-wise, move to one side and try
to look and not look at the same moment.
Is it clear (*er*) now? *Oh say can you see?*
The "Anthem for Doomed Youth" is a brief tracery.

It will be gone by the time you read this.

EARTH'S BURNT UMBER

After the Painting: Orange & Yellow.
Mark Rothko 1956

1.
Sun rise or set, the earth's
burnt umber
flames at the horizon,

fountaining. Red
heat, vengeful as the word
vermillion

rises into orange,
the most
hurtful color,

and *yellow yellow yellow* trills
relentless, noon-sound-singing
and unbearable.

2.
Dry earth, remember indigo repose:
sweet haze, your twilight-pitcher's pooling
gray-green curves, the damp-with-

droplets sheen, cerulean as the Past
when water lipped, blue,
everywhere, lavish as from a dipper,

silvery with plenitude, with amplitude,
thirst–quenching, liquid
word-song, spilling

promises of endless shade like
paintings from the Hudson Valley
and the Adirondack Schools.

3.
Instead, Mark Rothko, you give us your
orange and yellow painting,
rimmed by angry

rectangular scratching:
a twentieth century (1956)
post-war retaliation;

4.
and what is lost
rises everywhere, crimson,
eye-veined with recognition.

All the hues for *"hot."*
Blurred heat insists and parches,
leaching *glow* from *global/*

(*glowball?*) leaves behind the
ashen simmer, body's dulled
sienna.

5.
The way night falls
too quickly, blunt,
in the unendurable

tropics, the way
a desert of gold ochre
glare extinguishes

the earth's burnt
umber until, singed,
the stars are

6.
pitiless pricked holes
in a black unblinking
canvas. *Hold me.*

Women Wearing White

Women wearing white. Women who slip
through their lives like a cool ringed hand
held briefly to a hot forehead. Women
consumed by their own fevers. Women in the
white shush-shush of corridors,
a squish of crepe-soled shoes.

Women in white like unstained vestal virgins
sitting on a summer porch. Berry stains or
blood? Wash it out, wash it out with the hottest
water—or will that set it? The stain of a woman fading,
brazen wine once flung across a tablecloth.
Women waiting for their own white final
dresses. Is that a nurse we see, all dressed in
white, motioning us toward the Emergency Exit?

THAT LIGHT. THAT PHOTOGRAPH. THAT COUPLE

You stand together poised against a rock,
that photograph I never got to make.
Below the sea flares: telephoto take
on ocean, cliffs, on sky. We laugh and talk.
You lean against each other in the sun
this blue unshadowed day. Focusing, anyone
would pause to look, heart stopped by elegance
of angle, gesture, as in partnered dance:
a momentary longed-for balance the camera
might prolong, file under the word "remember";
the dream beyond the lived one, present tense,
fixed by the bright insistence of a lens.
Above your heads your long-limbed children climb,
change distance, frame and shutter speed, shift time.

Watercolor

walking along the river bank
the sky the color of smoke
the smoke the color of water:
even the grasses were smoky
and the river wound, dazed,
under a leavening sky.
sometimes a gray house passed us by
or did we pass it? no matter.
a whole day was in motion;
our river would mix with an ocean,
indistinguishable finally and
much further away.
the pale wash of seascape,
a matte-background sky, some
salt-spattered kisses: was
someone crying? was it the rain?
a flock of starlings sprinkled
emphatic pepper grains over
the expanse of wet paper
upon which a few clouds were
beginning to write themselves.

The Lost World

The Lost World

I had to make up the painting today
because you were no longer there to do it for me.
I had already left by the window;
the white-edged scrap of lace curtain the only thing left stirring.
The bed was beginning to reassume its own imprint;
the dewy lawn plushed back into place
and the sky, its clouds, eye-stroked, eye-
stroked itself blue-white like the story
of somebody's ancestors, pentimentoed.

I saw my life peeled away from its many layers.
Already the memories were flaking and cracking
and I could no longer be sure
exactly where you had stood
in relation to me, or what you had said,
nor the white layer of preparation that underlay
the whole picture. All that was unsaid,
left out or painted over would become the property
of the curators of the Memory Museum
to whom I bequeathed my entire estate.

As I mentioned, you had already gone before me
so the painting of "seeing and being seen"
which hopefully was the only thing we ever
could give each other was never completed.
I was still trying to memorize
those stippled meadow-flowers on canvas,
reproduce our lily pond at
daybreak, the thin pencil-trill
of scribbled birdsong and how
light drenched and sanctified.

Light everywhere! But
as I mentioned, you
had already gone before me,
leaving a vortex like Guernica,
the women looking back over their shoulders
while seeming to run forward.
Their noble jagged heads in profile
struggled against cubism: disjointed

jigsaw flight; cowled shawls, horse-
fright and all the wild-flung flailing
helpless against the current, sucking,
whirlpooled drownward
into the tunnel-mouth of loss,
foreshadowing this twenty-first century.

Pale Light in the Luxembourg Garden

A pale watery light invades the trees
as if one were already reading
the "Book of One's Life." —Afterwards.—
Was it like that? Was it really like that?
I remember holding you in my arms
but the etched intake of breath
has already faded, like a sepia photograph
in which posed strangers, frontal and solemn,
look out and beyond one, preternaturally still.

This season your lover is both
coming toward and receding. Tentative,
the bluish sky's an aquatint, a puff of breath
between stark sudden-springing branches.
All kinds of promises are not yet made,
diaphanous: hold on, hold back
before raw summer sears us in its blast

and irons down our (photocopied) past,
helplessly pressed
like leaves that blazed once, faraway,
emblemed in wax—(we had our day)—
between the pages of some dusty book
in which not even we, so faded now,
would ever care to look.

THEIR TRANQUIL LIVES

Oh lost world of Gustav Klimt,
the jeweled and doe-eyed women
swam the walls and ceilings
of pre-Holocaust Vienna's
ornate opera. Women's compliance
did not need to be stated,
was pink and white
and not hidden by drapes.

World War I had not yet happened.
The city was a beaker spilling over
with bits of gold applied
which one could drink
or pour into, carefully
lavish and lucky.

Outside the window apples
shone in their dappled garden.
The women had proud
names, and pregnancies.
They rose like mermaids through
their tranquil lives,
upward and passionate.
The insides of their wrists
were white and still unmarked,
smoothed with kisses:

Vienna before History—
Each morning was a waking: pond
drenched in light; the path,
perfumed with little flowers, stitched
white butterflies and the painter-god
creating first-words; a mosaic
of *forbidden*.

As if *memory*
would tapestry forever
voyeur-painter's studios, light-
drenched: the livid golden hair
and modeled arms and bracelets lifting:
perfect breasts; rounded nutcracker
thighs and, ready for the
taking, the ripe fruit.

As if the comet,
pleasure, would never
burn itself to ash; the dross,
once-glorious color
seeping, leaching, thinly
staining Europe.
Oh much punished and
lost worlds of Gustav
Klimt, while you stroked
undertone rose-ochre tints
to flesh, your century,
demented, waited
for its urgent re-inventions;
voice-over, take-over
newsreel/newsprint narratives:
blunt *black-and-white*

MOMA. NEW YORK CITY

It was vast, the renovated
Museum of Modern Art in New York City
in November. Nine/one/one
had already happened and the breeze
of buried voices, particles of
glitter, merely tickled
the bright air on West 53rd street.
New York was block-like, tiger mother
crouching over steaming subways
while overhead, gaiety flourished like a banner
as it does sometimes in New York,
lively & multicolored.

And in this new repository,
"Modern Art" rushed backward
faster than we could have imagined
through yawning galleries, hope chests
for an expected future. Oblivious,
Rousseau's *"The Sleeping Gypsy"*
drowsed on his slab of washed
museum wall; an Amulet:
cheek-pillowed, vibrant
cloak and trustful toes;
the trance-like lion-guarded pose
unaware of history and its many voices.

He slumbered as he had in 1955
when I first visited the museum.
Shuttered in that cool
twentieth-century sleep lab,
we studied dreaming through
the self-reflective glass
as if doing research
on how to become Sacred.
Now I stood, a Rip Van Winkle witness
to decades when glittering New
York was not postmodern yet;
before the bluff and beckon
broke attention outward.

And the sculpture garden
cried "Remember me?"
as if a rising tangle of wild cries
were not happening outside
and nothing had been obscured.
Monet's *"Nympheas"* for instance,
the pastel cloudy scrim of swirling pink
you'd never want to leave.
And Van Gogh's cocky dislocated
"Self Portrait"; its neck-craning stare
inquisitive, one swiveled eye
like the bloody yolk of an egg,
the lurid surface smeared with paint
as if we already knew *"The Ending."*

OWL CRY OVER ROME

From the clotted dark of the garden
the coagulating night, an owl called,
surprising the outspread town.
The feathery throat-flutter
vibrated, air-parting.

It made a sound like the word "forget,"
that evening, calling me to the window,
then on to the terrace, counting—
Did this mean someone would die?
and who? and when?

Then the air closed again, damp, gravid,
its thousands of mysteries: a pause,
until the longed-for cry came again, ululation—
like women mourning, or women's joy—
seven times reverberating over the

seven hills of Rome.
And then, the owl, like the
promise of "maybe"
continued calling from further away,
too palely etched to be heard
by sleepers oblivious within
houses in their futile restlessness.
"Forget, forget"—it juddered:
or was it *"Remember"?*

Tipping Point

How this soft green garden strokes
and soothes as we walk among her:
the brush tips of grasses feathering *paint me paint me;*
translucent mauve fingers of children
shifting sun's shadow, the certainty of light.

You know the descending moment, day's end,
dark ending I'm speaking of;
when the green glimmer inhales its fragrance, holds
an exact calibration, deliberate & slant-wise, the
breath-angle—you've seen it too—
making everything perfect and therefore unbearable.

That moment before the over-spilling pitcher is poured from,
when the sheen of droplets still shivers on its oval surface,
before liquid, brimming, melds with the Great River *Thirst*
and we, silver winged, lunar, are emptied and earthen—
I could love anyone right now: you, for instance.

BUTTON

The last time we saw her
she was waving from a doorway
of a boxcar gathering speed
and going east. The last time
we saw her she was carrying
a thin suitcase and a button
was missing from the sweater that
her mother knit: *goodbye, take care of
yourself.* When they took her
she was wondering *where why
why me?* and we were also,
helpless, straining to see beyond
a horizon we would only guess at as
we watched her, small & vanishing,
standing and looking out that one last
longing time at breathing blue-green fields.
And why didn't she turn
and run right out of the picture frame
back into our waiting arms
before it was too late, my late
great aunt, a last un-
noticed snip of history?

And that lost button, why
wasn't it sewn on tighter?

The Path Into Night

Two drawn out
calls of birds
falling in fifths
in late evening
and now the tree frogs
start to throb.
Solitude sinks in
like a blanket, bluish
absence inhaled; skin
a sheen of sadness
finely silver-edged.
If one's whole life
were to be this
solitary would the
true notes
start to sound;
repeated bird song
measuring darkness?